1

First published 2004
by

Mudfog Press
c/o Arts Development
The Stables
Stewart Park
The Grove
Marton
Middlesbrough
TS7 8AR

www.mudfog.co.uk

Cover design and print by
Archetype Tel: 08702 245 151

ISBN 1-899503-65-X

Acknowledgements:
Thanks to Craig Hornby for historical inspiration.
Thanks to my daughter Holly for helping me keep my words alive and to
Rebecca - for all your belief and support when I needed it most.

Sexy Baz's Birds, *The Wrong California* and *The Three O' Clock
Bubble* have appeared in Sand Magazine issue 1, *Eston Cemetery*
has appeared in *Smelter* (Mudfog 2003) and an earlier version
of *The Shaft* appeared in *Writearound Anthology 1989*. *Teesside
Requiem* was developed in performance at The Poetry Vandals,
Newcastle and the Hydrogen Jukebox, Darlington with music from
Sean Lennox and Rebecca Severi.

Mudfog Press is a member of
The Independent Northern Publishers
www.northernpublishers.co.uk

Mudfog gratefully acknowledges
the support of
Arts Council England
and Middlesbrough Borough Council

Welcome to

The wrong california

The Middlesbrough
Poet Laureate Poems
2003-2004

To Chris,
good luck in getting
a pamphlet.

Andy Willoughby

[signature]
2012

Dedicated to the memory of
my Grandmother Winifred Hellawell

(formerly Dawson, nee Robinson)

Foreword

The idea of a Poet Laureate for Middlesbrough first took shape during the Writearound Festival in 1998. Chosen through a competition open to people over 18, born, living or working in Middlesbrough, the local Poet Laureate would produce a series of poems inspired by people, places and events in and around the town during their year in office. The Laureate is encouraged to meet and work with various community groups, carry out some historical research and visit sites of social significance.

So far there have been four Middlesbrough Poet Laureates, each with a different voice and vision of their town: Ghazala Bashir, Pauline Plummer, Norah Hill and Andy Willoughby. All of them are featured in the Mudfog's 2003 poetry anthology *Smelter*.

Andy Willoughby comes from Grangetown and attended the Universities of Kent and Sheffield. He is co-director of The Hydrogen Jukebox Cabaret of the Spoken Word based at Darlington Arts Centre, co-editor of Ek Zuban Independent Publishers and currently Joint Writer in Residence at The University of Teesside. He also works as a freelance poet, director and playwright on various school and community projects. He has been published in *Oral* - an anthology of British performance poetry (Sceptre 1999) and *The Flesh of the Bear* - an anthology of poetry from South West Finland and North East England (Ek Zuban 2004).

This collection of poems gives a cross-section of Willoughby's eclectic writing, covering passionate performance pieces, popular football poems, seriously crafted formal verse and honed minimal observations. Within all of his work he retains an authentic Teesside voice, lilting from the back streets of a post-industrial landscape to a dying fall over Eston Hills.

A further collection, *Tough,* will be published by Smokestack later in 2005 and a collection of translated poems, *Poetry Killer,* is due to be published in Finland by Savukeidas in 2005.

Contents

The wrong california

The Wrong California

We come from the wrong California,
No-one but the ironmasters made their fortune here.
The masses that huddled here for work
Did not come for liberty but survival,
Though they dragged tons of stone
And Sydney Harbour Bridge from ancient hills
Amongst other wonders unacknowledged -
Just read the Dorman Long signs on the girders
Of the London Underground!
They formed their unions but found no myth of Zorro
And **"fuck off joe shite"** sprayed on a Grangetown wall
Does not speak of freedom with a Z but says it all;
We come from the wrong California,
Dream of cheap holidays, casual work and sweet football.

Sexy Baz's Birds

We were old enough and daft enough,

To think we could make it on three chords
And a crafty way with words,
Developed to get into teenage knickers
And save us from skinhead kick-ins,
The year somebody nicked Sexy Baz's birds
From the miraculous aviary out his back,
Walled by the cemetery with its large proportion
Of gadgies killed in accidents down the works -
Probably the thieving scumbag's point of entry
And escape with their loot of bright yellow canaries,
Various finches and amazing beaked lovebirds
Raised by Baz's guitar hands and trained to fly to
His tuneful whistle in perfect pitch that I could never manage.
But what the hell it's the passion that counts
Just ask Iggy and Johnny and Lou,
Never mind that it was Beatles retro we were into -
The only group we wanted to be was the best.
So in between the angry blasters in the hired church hall,
(Jesus, why is the monsignieur such a tight get,
Charging by the half hour, our last dole quids 'n'all?),
We tried to hit the harmonies of "It's only love
And that is all" but Baz mate it wasn't enough
To get us out of there or make us tough,
So when you said you thought you knew which thug
Had made off with your feathered babies
I said, "Let's go bray the truth outta the punk" -
Having seen Dirty Harry for the umpteenth time
On the new-fangled video and fancying our luck.
You said "Don't be daft, it's done and dusted"
And fiddled with a sad acoustic E– minor,
"Leave it man you'll get our heads smashed in."
Shortly after that I dreamed of you standing in the cemmy,
Devoid of its usual early teen bostick-sniffing cider-suckers:
You were singing "Nowhere Man" in Lennon mode

To the beats of a thousand brightly coloured wings
And the iron miners started bursting from their graves
Like the zombies in Thriller. It was our band's best moment,
I wasn't even in it, and though we hit various obscure stages
After that between post office, factory and college,
And shook them up but didn't find our Cavern spot,
Or shake the corners of this earth it never disappointed
Me as much as when I woke up and thought of your empty cage,
Knowing there was no way out without further knowledge
Of what brought us to this Beatle-murdering, bird-stealing age.

The Three O'Clock Bubble

Saturday Morning booze-dregged blues
6.30 a.m. and we're sure to lose

I'm staying in bed where it's safe and warm
But the three o'clock bubble begins to form

Bitter coffee, glass of resolve,
Sense of doom starts to dissolve

They're kicking in – the season's highs,
Now the three o'clock bubble begins to rise

Greasy spoon with Gaz and Ed
Fried egg dreams jump from head to head

I'm ready for a pint with stomach lined
The three o'clock bubble begins to shine

Fantasies of hometown pride -
Like childhood dreams had never died

Ten minutes to go, steak and kidney pie
The three o'clock bubble can really fly

Unspoken hopes between kids and dads
When we say nowt it's not so bad

There's hidden love in the songs of hate -
The three o'clock bubble radiates

Early goal explosion then relief
Eyes are lit with a new belief

Songs rise up and split grey skies -
The three o'clock bubble is dancing high

A change in play and silence reigns
The bated breath of a crowd in pain

A dim back pass and it's one all
The three o'clock bubble begins to fall

Second goal chipped from the halfway line
We're running out of luck and time

Their French genius puts us in the shade
The three o'clock bubble begins to fade

If we get one back - we live in hope
But fragile defences just can't cope

Ball hits the net and we're the worst
The three o'clock bubble has really burst

Post-match post-mortem downing beer
Continued sense of gut-wrenched fear

Forever doomed to be second-rate
As the three o'clock bubble disintegrates

Fear of falling and the deadly drop
Inspires some meatheads into kicking off

As flashing lights hit the rain-soaked streets
The ghost of the bubble glistens – then retreats.

Eston Cemetery

(i)

In the new section -
Shiny black marble,
Colour pictures inset,
Of rockin' Elvis Presley:
Flash cars and red guitars
Mark the early graves
Of quick young men,
Who never will be stars.

(ii)

Walking through the Sixties
Where the shattered sharp edges
Of hammered and battered tombstones
Fallen on the lush body of green grass
Lay where the vandals have cast them;
Living only in the moment of destruction,
Thinking nothing, caring nothing,
Numb with the days of nothing:
This is their silent declaration -
This is their wordless memorial,
The dead man's bones are dust.

(iii)

Turning your pram to shield
Your eyes from the warm Easter sun
Your mind is grabbed at by colour:
The blooming daffodils on older graves
Well-tended flowers on the new arrivals,
William's softly soothing balm of nature;
When I offer you, five months old,
A stray broken glowing blossom
You reach out, grasp and giggle,
Beguiled by the newness of yellow.

(iv)

There is a certain unnamed stillness
Here in the heart of the cemetery
Draping old mossy sandstone graves
With no fresh flowers to mark fresh loss.
The ramshackle grafittied chapel,
With its aerosol litanies of hate and hurt
From boiling virgins and sad chalk lovers,
Decays unmourned in a grey green corner
Though its ancient Norman foundations
And heavy boned seventeenth century bricks
Refuse to rot away to nothing:
The lemon sunlight of blustery March
Catches its stones in leaf dappled shadows,

While the weathered markers of iron miners
Crumble slowly like the winter minds
Of those who can still remember them.

The Shaft

Below us tin rooftops of a derelict farm:
Brown of bricks, darks of clover and moss
Fade as you dance into my clumsy arms.
Buzzing flies serenade us as we find loss,

Papal moral certainties burst fast
Like ripe bilberries in our mouths,
Summer rhythms overcome belief,
As we roll around North to South,

Far above the abandoned caverns,
That hold the secrets of family past:
Worked-out whale bellies of stone.
Where those ancestors paid the cost

Of migrant dreams of better lives,
Inside hills that echo wordless shock,
From the lost souls of men and boys
Killed in falls of blue-veined rock.

Questions chime from the concealed shaft
Where pickaxes ring from lost decades,
Pricking our bubble of pastoral shade
With hard iron probing of identity.

We discover our answers in a rich seam
Of words not given freely but excavated.
Twisted into drills by our love and dreams
Our needs find new meaning in tumbling blue,

Sudden judder of falling syllables
Onto our desperate searching tongues,
Revealing to us a ladder of descent
Leading to the nameless bottom rungs -

Where lost faces tattooed with bitter dust
Pockmarked with steel-hard silent pride,
Shift embarrassed and once more subside
Into the hills where our lust is satisfied.

Teesside Requiem

The papers this week carry half familiar faces
In sentimentalist and sensationalist headlines.
One's a wasted boy's, the other's a football ace's.
Only one will get black armbands during the nation's halftimes,
The other tut-tuts from concerned tea-time mothers
At the opium wolf blowing at our post-industrial door

It's a shipyard siren
It's the steelworks hum
It's the sound of a crowd that needs a win
It's a broken needle on a violin
It's the sound of a Teesside requiem

The Golden Boy dances with his hands held out flat,
Inner radar as he weaves his magic and his folktale.
Nowhere Lad nods out on the nothing horse,
His kicked habit's lapse made his heart fail.
I try to concentrate on South Bank's dancing lad
Leaping over six-feet defenders like a salmon

It's a shipyard siren
It's the steelworks hum
It's the sound of a crowd that needs a win
It's a broken needle on a violin
It's the sound of a Teesside requiem

Georgie Best superstar dragged Nana back to Ayresome,
Twenty-odd years after the little man's heyday.
She'd heard he was the best this country's seen:
Said she had to watch "El Beatle" play,
Grudgingly accorded him greatness but didn't concede -
Our Wilf was still installed in her stadium of dreams

It's a shipyard siren
It's the steelworks hum
It's the sound of a crowd that needs a win
It's a broken needle on a violin
It's the sound of a Teesside requiem

Sometimes it seemed he had the power of flight,
Skimming like a swallow inches from the surface.
Black and white film shows him kicking tennis balls
Round Slaggy Island's alleys just like so many kids ,
Just like we did on St. Peter's muddy Catholic fields;
Nowhere Lad's face looms up at me like a lead balloon.

It's a shipyard siren
It's the steelworks hum
It's the sound of a crowd that needs a win
It's a broken needle on a violin
It's the sound of a Teesside requiem

It's the freckled face of a lost boy happy in green hills,
Running wildly stained purple at the mouth,
Been popping bilberries instead of pills,
Smokeless wind in his face from the south.
No doubt he dreamed of being the next Boro legend,
Like Nana's tiny man who ran rings around Scots giants,

It's a shipyard siren
It's the steelworks hum
It's the sound of a crowd that needs a win
It's a broken needle on a violin
It's the sound of a Teesside requiem

Teesside rightly mourns its most famous son,
Remembering his frail figure waving from twin towers
As we stood enthralled on Wembley way,
Security guards speechless at the respectful adulation
For the white-haired chap they didn't recognise.
Immortality brings thousands out as his hearse rolls by

It's a shipyard siren
It's the steelworks hum
It's the sound of a crowd that needs a win
It's a broken needle on a violin
It's the sound of a Teesside requiem

We will not record the Nowhere Lad's demise,
To be passed down like well-worn wisdom
Through generation to generation in football ground asides.
Only an estranged mother's tears will salt this passing,
Before we move to the next shock-horror headline- fanfare,
Then Nowhere Lad will be relegated to nowhere

It's a shipyard siren
It's the steelworks hum
It's the sound of a crowd that needs a win
It's a broken needle on a violin
It's the sound of a Teesside requiem.

Elementis Exchange

Kalle says the Elementis Chromium factory
Will make a great sci-fi B-movie set
As I show him its dark green grimness,
Its gleaming streamline deco centrepiece.

Post-nuclear Teesside's mutated descendants
Will sacrifice their enemies and children
In the hungry chromium vats
To appease an angry boss god,

Like our forefathers sentenced to death
For the gods of profit and metals,

Oh Elementis your beautiful reflecting curves
Will linger in Finnish poet's dreams,
Like your legacy in workers' lungs.

Bride of the Tees (Kiplingesque)

She's trained her body with Arabian rhythms,
Beaten out on battered old drums,
She makes her stomach rumba and ripple,
Belled ankles shimmy as the lute player strums,

Bride of the Tees,
On "Taste of Arabia" tables,
Dancing the cold river warm,
Rocking the wild waters calm,
And the cooling towers pipe up their own music,
And the cranes dance metal ballets at dawn;

They all dance metal ballets at dawn,

Smoking strawberry flavours from hookahs,
Poets of Teesside and Turku entranced,
As the Bride of the Tees to hand-clapping
Burns their eyes with a hot belly dance,

Bride of the Tees,
Freed by infusion of cultures,
From lands far to the east of Teesport,
Lands with their own kind of sport,
Hammers a rhythm out barefoot,
Hypnotic as a Lapp shaman's beat,
And northern streets blaze with Arabian heat;

They all blaze with Arabian heat.

The Ghost of an Egg (for Holly)

Dim gleams of light bounced off Mr Trayer's bald head,
As his cache of ghost stories thrilled us on rainy mornings,
Where the Dorman's airy bird room exhibited the stuffed
Corpses of numerous gulls, beaks open in warning.
His whispered weird tales transformed the mundane:
He could open the family wardrobe into hell's portal,
An old kettle could steam with vengeful voices,
And every story would come to a bloodcurdling scream;
The stories kept our motley Saturday club crew
In good-humoured order as we dissected sharks,
Polished quartz and moonstone, collected strange fungi
From Albert's great park with its old men from Lowry.
Our childhoods made precious by natural knowledge
Given by a man who probably did it for nothing.
The museum's done up for the millennium now
Thirty years on from tank tops and glam rock,
The tatty old lion is the town's affectionate totem
Of days when cases haphazardly offered you treasures.
Trayer's gone but he's left a legacy for the others and me,
Who bring our kids here and name stinkhorn and puffball
In the old park and outlying forests, know the difference
Between oak, beech, sycamore and chestnut,
Though we come from a town famous for smoke
In the national media's one-eyed cartoon perception.
We are connected to the world outside the ring of iron
And see ghosts in the stones and cracks of old buildings.
In the bright new exhibition with my daughter
I feel my childhood's own spirit hungry for knowledge,
Thrilled by spectres and lurking shadow monsters,
Try to transmit the feeling without being a bore:
In the too small corner that celebrates the town's iron
I fail to get over how many souls remained in the hills
For the wealth of the man this place is named after,
With relief pull back the cases in the unchanging bird room

Revealing the pinned cadavers of numerous insects,
A dinosaur egg and gleaming, blown eggshells:
Their light brings me the spirit of kind Mr Trayer,
Later, as I watch her sleeping after the bedtime story,
The ghosts of the unknown and half forgotten
From the old museum's cases fly on phantom feathers,
Circling the space between now and then,
Between sleep and dream time,
Circling.

Ride the Red Dragon
(for Dad and for the Boro)

(i)

128 years up
    in fireworks
        red flags waving
for Teesside pride
    we are red dragon riding
        in the land of brains and bards
high as the bubble that for once
    hasn't burst
getting our gobs around the strange word:
    winners.

(ii)

Ultramarine is my favourite colour,
Also known as Yves Klein blue,
Induces an electric vibe of calm,
When my mind is boiling crimson

and red is the colour of my team

The fields in Kent where I learned
The endless shades of combined words
Were green as my springtime love:
I longed for cooling tower silhouettes

and red was the colour of my team

The packages from home were brown,
Crackling with anticipation of results,
Mam sent every kick from our dirty old town,
Desperate for news that we could survive

and red was the colour of my team

Royal blue swathed the iron lady
As the shipyards swiftly closed,
Chimneys and furnaces crashing down,
The queues grew longer for signing on

and red was the colour of my team

Black was the doom toll print,
Announcing the Boro's demise,
Grey padlock on Ayresome gates
Like a skinhead kick in the guts

and red was the colour of my team

Multi-coloured newspapers arrived,
Pronounced tacky by the chattering class:
The scarlet shirts were my phoenix,
I have always read the paper backwards

and red was the colour of my team

Yellow gold was the whiskey glass,
In late night bedsits after waiting shifts,
To ill-mannered gents in penguin suits,
Who believe work's a matter of the will

and red was the colour of my team

In Japan the rice was purest white,
On Tatami floors I dreamed of home,
The papers kept arriving monthly,
Reminding me of who I'd been

and red was the colour of my team

White were the towers of Wembley,
With Dad breathing hard with angina,
As his childhood dreams dissolved,
For the third time in cockney blue

and red was the colour of my team

Silver shone the surgeon's knife,
That restored him for this final day,
Where a century of battered pride
Rides the red dragon and flies away

and red is the colour of my team.

(iii)

The stadium roof is closed at Cardiff,
We are Romans at the Coliseum,
Doing battle by proxy with history
That has by tradition struck us dumb

With a century and a half of toil
In industry that cripples and kills,
We raise family to face the tale
Of dormant furnaces and empty hills,

So our singing has a desperate joy
As it strains the metal ceiling,
Our ghosts rise up from within
In the final whistle's flood of feeling.

Not 'only football' this hard won identity,
This generations-spanning mind-flash
Of public memory and personal past,
These many thousand exhaled at lasts,

We'll win nowt and we'll take the pain,
With grim wit and some graveyard craic,
When the Boro let us down again,
Was the mantra of all our grandparents,

All changed now as we take the silverware,
In a kaleidoscope of memory through tears,
Wilfy, Robbo, Big John and dead relatives
Flash before us as a second fills with years.

My father and uncle both speak to their Dad
"We did it at last – won in our lifetime!"
Generations of ghosts ride the red dragon
Through the roof and into this rhyme.

It's not just a game but life's very fabric:
Though this town deserves respect never given
For the steel structures that girdle the globe,
We'll take this cup as our symbol of hope.

Volleying the Invisible

We played football in the gloaming,
Enacting home international glories,
Not even stopping with the sunset
When the ball disappeared into deadlight,

I still hear the backbeat of your kick
And the echo of my swung anticipation,
You're England and I'm Northern Ireland -
Being the better fighter you take the lion's choice,

But I improved there in the darkness,
Listening intensely for the unseen.
Today I haven't lost that precious habit,
Though if I were to strike the ball now

It would end up in older hands:
Work worn red or laced with scars,
While mine are pale pen pushers,
Still striving for that sweet connection

Our feet made from beat to striking beat,
Although we never meet these days,
John, I still strive to impress you -
Volleying the invisible into imagination's net.